# NEW SERIES!
## Basic Biographies

**Reading Level: Grade 1**
**Interest Level: Grades Pre-K-2**
This series features easy-to-read text and carefully chosen photos that highlight key moments of the subjects' lives.
Publisher: The Child's World • Discount: 30% off list
Binding: Reinforced Library • Size: 9¹/₂ x 8 • Pages: 24
Features: Full-Color & B&W Photographs, Web Sites, Glossary, Index

| | | | |
|---|---|---|---|
| ____ | **CWK126** | **BASIC BIOGRAPHIES (8 vols.)** | **119.60** |
| ____ | CW3387 | ●Albert Einstein/Kesselring, Spr 10 | 15.95 |
| ____ | CW3394 | ●Barack Obama/Kesselring, Spr 10 | 15.95 |
| ____ | CW3400 | ●Charles Schulz/Amoroso, Spr 10 | 15.95 |
| ____ | CW3417 | ●Helen Keller/Amoroso, Spr 10 | 15.95 |
| ____ | CW3424 | ●Jackie Robinson/Amoroso, Spr 10 | 15.95 |
| ____ | CW3431 | ●Michelle Obama/Kesslering, Spr 10 | 15.95 |
| ____ | CW3448 | ●Rosa Parks/Amoroso, Spr 10 | 15.95 |
| ____ | CW345X | ●Thomas Edison/Kesselring, Spr 10 | 15.95 |

**BASIC BIOGRAPHIES**

# Michelle Obama

by Susan Kesselring

Michelle Obama is the **First Lady** of the United States. She is married to the **president**, Barack Obama.

Michelle Obama is the First Lady of the United States.

Michelle was born on January 17, 1964. She grew up in Chicago, Illinois. She has one big brother, Craig.

Michelle and her mom are very close.

Michelle was very smart in school. She loved to learn.

This is Michelle when she was in elementary school.

When she got older, Michelle went to **college**. She became a **lawyer**. There were not very many black lawyers at that time.

This is Michelle when she finished college.

Michelle wanted things to be fair for all people. She knew that the color of a person's skin did not matter. She worked to make things fair.

Michelle has always wanted to help people.

Michelle met Barack at work. They went on a date to a movie. After more dates, they fell in love and got married.

This is Michelle and Barack at their wedding.

Michelle and Barack had a daughter, Malia. Before long, they had another daughter named Sasha.

Malia (left) is three years older than Sasha (right).

In 2009, Barack became the forty-fourth president. Michelle became First Lady. Barack and Michelle are the first black president and First Lady.

Michelle and Barack danced together the night Barack became president.

Michelle still works hard to help people. She works with kids in schools. She helps families that have little money.

Michelle tries to make people's lives better.

Michelle is very busy as First Lady. But she loves to be with her daughters. She says her most important job is being Malia and Sasha's mom.

Michelle takes care of her family.

# Glossary

**college (KOL-ij):** College is a school people go to after high school. Michelle went to college.

**First Lady (FURST LAY-dee):** The wife of the president of the United States is the First Lady. Michelle is the First Lady.

**lawyer (LOY-ur):** A lawyer is someone who helps others understand laws. Michelle worked as a lawyer.

**president (PREZ-uh-dent):** The president is the leader of the United States. Barack became the president.

# To Find Out More

## Books

Boswell, John. *The Barack & Michelle Obama Paper Doll & Cut-Out Book*. New York: St. Martin's Griffin, 2009.

Edwards, Roberta. *Michelle Obama: Mom-in-Chief*. New York: Penguin, 2009.

Hudak, Heather C. *Michelle Obama*. New York: Weigl, 2009.

## Web Sites

Visit our Web site for links about Michelle Obama: *childsworld.com/links*

Note to Parents, Teachers, and Librarians: We routinely verify our Web links to make sure they are safe and active sites. So encourage your readers to check them out!

# Index

# About the Author

**Susan Kesselring** has taught all ages of children from preschool through grade 8. She has been a certified Reading Recovery teacher and director of a preschool. She loves to help children get excited about learning. Family, friends, books, music, and her dog, Lois Lane, are some of her favorite things.

On the cover: Michelle Obama waved to the crowds when her husband became president on January 20, 2009.

Published by The Child's World®
1980 Lookout Drive • Mankato, MN 56003-1705
800-599-READ • www.childsworld.com

ACKNOWLEDGMENTS
The Child's World®: Mary Berendes, Publishing Director
The Design Lab: Design and production
Red Line Editorial: Editorial direction

PHOTO CREDITS: Jae C. Hong/AP Images, cover, 16, 22; Sándor F. Szabó/iStockphoto, cover; Sara D. Davis/AP Images, 3; Ted S. Warren/AP Images, 5; Polaris, 7, 9, 11; AP Images, 13; Vandell Cobb/AP Images, 15; Pablo Martinez Monsivais/AP Images, 17; Manuel Balce Ceneta/AP Images, 19; Evan Vucci/AP images, 21

Printed in the United States of America in Mankato, Minnesota.
November 2009
F11460

LIBRARY OF CONGRESS CATALOGING-IN-PUBLICATION DATA
Kesselring, Susan.
  Michelle Obama / by Susan Kesselring.
    p. cm. — (Basic biographies)
  Includes index.
  ISBN 978-1-60253-343-1 (library bound : alk. paper)
 1. Obama, Michelle—Juvenile literature. 2. Presidents' spouses—United States—Biography—Juvenile literature. 3. Legislators' spouses—United States—Biography—Juvenile literature. 4. African American women lawyers—Illinois—Chicago—Biography—Juvenile literature. 5. Chicago (Ill.)—Biography—Juvenile literature I. Title. II. Series.
 E909.O24K47 2010
 973.932092—dc22 [B]                                    2009029597